Listening to Silence

POEMS, PRAYERS & SUPPLICATIONS

REV. LUIS CALDEIRA

ISBN-10: 0615564070

ISBN-13: 9780615564074

Acknowledgements

To my dear Almar Sator and to my Beloved,
the One that Remains,

My Mystical Christ.

Foreword

Within each of us, there is an intuitive, deep, and abiding hunger for an Essence greater and more powerful than we can imagine and more loving than we have ever experienced. We innately possess a profound capacity and yearning for what we know to be Holy. I believe we are created with a spark of the Divine within, and we long to become one with the Whole, the Essence, the Fire.

Through my adult life, on my own spiritual pilgrimage, I have read numerous books guiding me into the practice of silence. I have had my own favorite writers whose thoughts and reflections provide encouragement and inspiration for the journey into my inner being and Holy Mystery. I truly love the experience of silence and contemplation! However, I must continue to be challenged to stop, get quiet, be still, breathe, and make myself silently available to be deeply connected with the Holy One.

I have had the joy and privilege of assisting Luis Caldeira with the editing of • *Listening to the Silence.* • We have sat side by side in front of the words he has written, taking turns reading aloud his beautiful and profound expressions of deep and honest pain, wisdom and healing, gifts given to him as a result of his journey and commitment to meditative and prayerful silence. Together, we have entered into • the Silence, • reading very slowly, breathing deeply, as when he originally wrote the words. I have been profoundly moved! We have laughed; we have cried; we have sighed. Amazingly, almost every time we have sat together in the editing process, we have come upon some written expression which touched deeply some issue with which one of us was struggling! A mystical gift! And I must say that now, Luis Caldeira has become one of my favorite writers and guides into the Great Mystery for Whom I yearn. His depth of wisdom, his way of honestly and tenderly speaking his own pilgrimage is healing and full of Holy Mystery. As you read and ponder the poems and beautiful prose of • *Listening to the Silence,* • read them slowly, with your breathing slow and deep, and simply breathe them in. Your spiritual life will be inspired and enriched, and you will, no doubt, know that you are not alone on your own walk with the Holy.

— Jan C. Lundy
Retired Psychotherapist, Spiritual Director

Introduction

In this collection of meditations, poems, sighs and songs, we discover our own relationship to loss, love, silence, existence, breathing, becoming, friendship, and listening. As Luis shares his own breathing with us, we can enrich our life by breathing with him. The book is a breathe. Read it • in and out. •

I have known Luis for many years, as a healer, poet and friend. Our work together in healing has been an important part of my own transformation. He intuitively integrates the mental, emotional, and physical in all processes. His poetry reflects this integration. Luis has a commitment to others that calls him forth into life. He prepares his own soul daily for his work, and he is a stand that people have the opportunity to transform.

Knowing Luis has been one of the blessings in my life. His life of learning is translated into opportunities for others, and this book of poetry is but one way he shares himself. • Listening to Silence • is a daily practice that creates new openings in life. My daily practice now includes a reading in this book.

— Kathleen Hudson,Ph.D.
Schreiner University/English Dept.

Listening to Silence

Poems, Prayers & Supplications

REV. LUIS CALDEIRA

❧ THE WRATH ☙

Sweet brother, the branches of your tree are most lovely when the generosity of their shade blesses us all,
But most unbecoming when used as a whip of your wrath.
Find the peace within your soul, sweet brother, and allow the bearing of her fruits to shine your preciousness.

❦ PRESENCE ❧

My Beloved
I'm here
Steady
Still
Yours
Again
I'm here.

❧ HONEY ❧

Does my gratitude go to the honey or the bee
The flower or the pollen
The soil or the rain
The sun or the moon
Fret not, sweet brother, for with an open heart one can remain grateful
to it all
They are all the paintings of the Great Master,
The One.

❦ UNION ❦

Praise me not, sweet brother,

For the light that you recognize in me, it is yours indeed,

Praise instead the Lover and Creator of Life,

For light He demanded and light came forth,

that you and I find Him in each other.

❦ The Eternal Seeker ❧

I went through temples and synagogues,

I went through churches and mosques,

To wise man, and medicine man I asked,

Where would I find You?

In blissful agony to my knees I fell,

You were nowhere to be found,

Then and there in listening to silence,

In my desperate sobbing You revealed Yourself,

Deep, deep within the vastness of my heart,

I didn't want to stop crying while laughter took over me.

❦ HUMANITY ❦

Contemplate not your wordily treasures

But your very essence, sweet brother

Bless me with your smile

Bless me with your tears

Better yet, bless me with your suffering that I may be one with you

And by the Blessed One,

Celebrate your humanness

for your unique brand of religion

might wedge a canyon between our souls,

And God will cry

And He will not cry alone.

☙ THE DANCE ❧

In waves of awe I dance
I let the silence of my heart rise upon the clouds of destiny only to
come faced with Your smile
I know You
You know me better
In our dance we create this moment
I look foolish dancing alone
I smile Your smile
For I know I'm not.

❦ LOVER ❦

I breathe.
Multiple loves
Like rain drops
I've fallen in love a hundred million times
So many lives
And the life was only One
You my sweet Beloved
In my millions of breaths
In Your windows of soul
I've fallen in love with You over and over
As I am again.

❧ YOUR GRACE ❧

I wonder if it was fate.

Can destiny be measured in time

And a second be counted as infinity?

In Your gaze, are my words Your scripture?

If I counted all the breaths taken, can I recognize them as Your ultimate offer?

Indeed.

And under Your gaze I am but a graceful lily,

A calm willow,

My breath, their gentle movement under the sun and the moon,

Fate? yes it remains

Eternity, this very second as my eyes read the book of life within me.

❦ Movement ❦

Have I cut the tree of life?
And if so
Have I fallen for the tree of knowledge?
If rivers of soul flow through
And gardens of heaven's colors blind me
Shall I keep drinking their waters
And shall I bathe in the beauty of all eternity?
Of course I will.
For I'll become the very ashes that will nurture trees and rivers,
Gardens and spirit.
I'm honored.

❧ THE JUDGE ❧

How often you speak of sin with your lips

And judgment with your heart

Only to find yourself in an all-around mirror room.

When is it that the value is most precious?

One, once a rock or a diamond?

And does not the diamond suffer the cutting of his facets?

Can I deny the beauty of whatever rock the Master has created?

It is then that I find the sin you so speak

and the judgment you so offer

Is the absence of the Divine.

I cry for you, I cry for myself

For I often open the door of that room

and see myself all around,

Rock in one hand,

Diamond in another.

৯ ALMIGHTY ৯

All that is new does become old
All that is old does eventually fade away
But You remain here,
Always have, always will stay.

❧ Blindness ❧

I collected experiences as if they were jewels,

And they were,

I did not recognize it as such

My blindness was behind the drive

I walked insistently in the narrow margins of despair

Where the Divine grew further into the depth of my imposing created

mountain,

Than I sat

And wept,

In each shed tear the mountain grew smaller

As the Master voiced, "I moved it."

And now I am, just am, and He continues to be in me.

❧ ECSTASY ❧

I fall to my knees in the mud,
My garments spattered,
I fall completely in it,
I roll in the mud as a wild animal,
Cup my hands with the dirt, cover my face with it,
I see my reflection in a puddle,
I don't recognize myself,
I'm happy now,
For I achieved perfection,
I can only see You.

❧ Surrender ❧

I grew to like it here,

This place of no place,

This abundance of nothingness,

I'm transparent,

I become,

I surrender,

I know that I don't know,

And that's enough.

❧ TRUDGING ❧

It was simple to reach for the cup,

How challenging it was to remain holding it,

From the coolest waters,

The heaviest loads,

I drink.

I carry.

I drink some more, for the load is becoming lighter.

꧁ AWAKENING ꧂

Hold the hand of the Master,

Close your eyes and smile,

Your path is now open,

And you shall walk with purpose,

Let your rocks from your past turn to diamonds,

Be the drop of dew in the ocean

And become the ocean,

Close your eyes and smile,

Almost there, is now, and now, the Beloved has revealed His secret to

you,

Yes, He hid Himself deep in the depth of your ocean

So go, go, sweet brother, and become that drop of dew again.

❧ ETERNAL TEMPLE ❧

My sweet brother ran to me crying:
•They closed the temple, they closed the temple, I came to be with the
Beloved and the temple is closed.•
He fell upon my arms,
I gave him two kisses on his cheeks, and placed my head on his chest.
•I just kissed the Beloved.• I said to him •His heart speaks to me of
eternity•
And so it was that the temple has always been open,
We rejoiced, we prayed.

❦ BOOK OF LIFE ❦

Write me with your darkest ink,

In this parchment paper of a open soul You know of my ignorance.

I claim no knowledge,

I'm but a poor spirit willing to be transformed in your writings.

The Sun blinds me, and I keep on trudging in the closed darkness.

Stones know You better than I,

I kiss them in gratitude; You have give them life

Write me, and burn the pages of this seeker

I desire nothing more but to be one with Your fire.

❧ EXISTENCE ❧

I've been writing Your names with my red blood in Your rose petals,
I drink from Your cup of fire that cleanses the way,
I've been rocked in Your cradle of redeeming love,
In the apocalypse of Your silence I found my silence Your silence
I've become the open lotus,
In Your deeper ponds I sleep,
In Your loud existence I awake.

❧ BEING ❧

I'm here, said the leaf to the branch.

I'm here, said the branch to the trunk.

I'm here, said the trunk to the roots.

I'm here, said the roots to the soil.

I'm here, said the tree to the sun.

Yes, you are there, said the sun to the tree.

Be shade my dear, be shade, for your blessings are who you are.

❧ HEALING ❧

The flower and the hummingbird shared a kiss,
God shed tears of joy,
The rainbows came full circle and healing was spread into the heart of
men.
I was there,
I saw it,
I was the hummingbird,
I was the flower,
I became the healing,
I was borne out of the joy that ran in God's face.

❦ RETURN OF INNOCENCE ❦

More than a lover of light,
A light in himself;
More than a flame,
A fire himself,
In the return of innocence,
The sweet death of knowledge,
As an infant I come,
As an infant I travel,
The path remains that of the Mystery,
In light and fire I make my nest,
The Eagle of Life keeps on sheltering this vulnerable soul,
I close my eyes now,
I rest,
I'm still.

❧ REMEMBRANCE ❧

In remembrance of sorrow
I shed a tear
In celebration of joy
I shed a thousand
I'm empty now
May the nectar of your Infinite Presence fill this cup
Tears are now part of that ocean where the salt and You become I AM.

❧ LAMENT ❧

What freedom
The embrace of the lament
The facing of the gift
Pearls in closing oceans
The foam of the ultimate awakening
I am whole
Complete
Understood
Became vulnerable in the wings of desperation
To rise as a roaring lion
Flying eagle
In the stillness of this quiet, subtle, innocent moment.
O sweet Beloved, I am grateful.

❧ NOTHINGNESS ❧

Yes, my nothingness is nothing indeed,
Neither do I seek the honey nor crave the salt,
The mild and the harsh have evaporated,
The solid and the gasses became mere thoughts,
Evil and goodness are but words in a lost perception.
Could death be so sublime?
So it is, the Mystery of Life in her unfolding beauty.

❦ UNSEEN MYSTERY ❦

The falcon within has resumed his flight,

The snake within uncoiled to her newest freedom,

The wolf within has merged with the moon,

The mother bear within rests her head from the longing of spring,

The desert within is vast,

The seasons are callings,

The months are teachers,

Days are moments,

Nights are breaths.

I sit, I think, I stop, I breathe, I live,

All of it! and nothing of me but the One to which, in all, I belong,

With that One my soul has fallen in love,

You sweet One, The Unseen Mystery.

❦ ETERNAL FIRE ❧

Invisible roots of mine sank into an invisible earth
Distant dreams submerged in waters of deeper oceans
Lost breaths became horizons in the turn of the winds
At last I was consumed by the Eternal Fire.

❧ SEERS OF LIFE ❧

O dancer of agony,
To You I must say Yes.
O seducer of suffering,
To You I must say Yes.
O charmer of desperation,
To You I must say Yes.
O player of darkness,
To You I must say Yes.
For in all of you, the seers of life,
I found the Golden Light of my Beloved.
Yes, then, I've bowed to You in gratitude.
And Yes I shall say.

❦ BLINDNESS ❧

You have embraced your story with all that you are
Your story stole your truth
You bled, and you graveled,
Your crying claims have fallen into an empty abyss,
Call yourself loud, sweet brother
Evoke the name of the Almighty
For your blindness has taken the Fire away from your heart
And self pity is unbecoming - even in the desert of solitude.

❦ REALIZATION ❧

-How is it over there, sweet brother?

- I am sorry, I cannot tell you.

- I often fantasize being there.

- One can only arrive here organically.

- So how is it that you can respond to my questions?

- Your desires have blinded you, have they not? One may call me your God consciousness, fulfill your destiny and I will embrace you from this reality.

- I long for You.

- But I am within you, sweet one.

❦ MOTHER ❦

I became a mother,
And nourished this child within that is me,
Cared for him,
Cradled him
Loved him and healed him,
I allow him to be the Seed of the Beloved,
The Divine Sun that shines through,
The living and loving hope,
That heals within me,
That heals within you,
I became a mother.

꧁ Holy Waters ꧂

In the vastness of Your unseen ocean,

I was salt vanishing in the presence of Your Holy Waters,

My nothingness transpires,

My will surrenders,

I am the lamb,

My sacrifice, the sweetness of Your mercy,

With You I, too, become eternal.

❧ THE BEGGAR ☙

I quiet the beast
I quiet the judge
I quiet the boaster
Knowledge avails me nothing
Experiences avail me nothing
Riches avail me nothing.
In the wilderness of silence, faced with Your splendor,
I'm a beggar,
I'm a fool,
I'm a child,
And so as a child I come to You in my innocence,
Pleading forgiveness and kissing Your everlasting sweetness,
My Beloved, my Master, my Christ.

❦ BURNING ❧

Devouring the infinite
Merging in stillness
That Your fire be abundant within me
I've been the sailor
And the carpenter
The farmer and the fisherman
And all along who knew that in all my traveling
I would find You within me?
I burn now
I burn immensely
I now sit and let it be.

❧ LIGHTING THE WAY HOME ☙

What rain may fall
What wave may crash
What oceans may swell
This Fire can't be extinguished
This burning will be the light by which I'll lead my sweet brother home.

❧ Dark Nights of the Soul ❧

What spiritual nights!
The rose that hides her petals,
The seed that recoils,
The flame under deep waters,
The untold healing story,
It is there,
It is there.
Let me bow to you O Great Unseen,
Let me create a river with my tears,
Let me build a castle with my longing,
It is here,
It is here.
I continue finding You in the darkest places of my existence
What precious nights!

❦ ESSENCE ❧

Seek no need to please your Divine,

For He that adores you and created your very existence in His very
essence is complete.

So please Him not, but be pleasing to Him in your Love towards His
Children.

Words are sweet, actions sweeter,

Be the honey of His comb in the hands of the seekers,

All pleasing is complete as His very essence.

❧ EXISTENCE ❧

Existence is not existence in Your absence
And Your absence never is.
The seed and the pomegranate
The fish and the water
The sun and the moon
You and I.
What simple fool can I be by forgetting to say thank you.
Thank You.

❧ Enough ❧

I'll pick you this delicate rose

- No need, I created it there for you.

I'll carve you a magnificent statue

- No need, use the wood to warm you.

I'll fast and pray and mediate all moments of my awakening times.

- No need, use your time to share your love.

I'll be anything you want me to be.

- O but you are, my child, you are, just as you are, enough.

❦ DIVINITY ❦

Recognize the Divine Face
There in the reflection of that pond
In the windows of your soul
In the smile of your loving care
Be it.
Be. Just be.
For you are God within, and I have God within
Because we share the Almighty
Let's not lose Him, just by telling.

❦ THE BOW ❦

I am the canvas under the Beloved brush
I am the melody that emanates from His music sheet
I am the seagull, wings supported by His loving wind
I am the empty pot where His wine will rest,
I just allow the Truth to emerge and bow to all suffering.
I am nothing, and I rejoice.

❧ Love Affair ☙

When having a love affair with death, one cannot have a love affair with
life, sweet brother.
It's not our fault if the rose looses her innocence
As it isn't our fault if ours was taken away.
The sun may refuse to shine but it's there
Your gentle beauty and joy may be covered by hurt and tiredness,
But it's there,
And in there, your Divine Self lives,
And in there, there's eternal life,
And for all that it's worth,
It's the best love affair I ever had.

ℰ WORTH ℛ

Why so feverishly insist in being some sort of something
If one's freedom is found in our utter nothingness?
Breathe, sweet brother, breathe
Find the Beloved in the space between, and rejoice in your meekness
Be the wings of the firefly
Be the foam on the shore
Be the rain drop on a leaf
And become the Fire of the Almighty.

❧ THE UNFOLDING ❧

Another layer
A bit deeper, not so gentle
Ah, the bittersweet taste of truth
It was God, it is God
Of course it is.
Who else or what else would open the wounds of our imperfections
only to love us the more?
Ever so silently, so lovingly He continues to whisper
•I love you too much to leave you there where you are right now•
The path is long, how precious that is,
For layer upon layer, oasis is revealed.
I'm in awe.

❦ PERSISTENCE ❦

What path have I chosen?
Rebellion dogs tear my flesh at every step
The molasses of sickness suffocates my every thought
The days become nights and nights turn to prisons of stillness
The breath is slow, heavy and burdened
Am I to find the Beloved somewhere?
I was told He lives in here
I'll let the Silence keep on guiding me.

❧ PERFECTION ❧

Whatever noises, they are noises
Sounds, beats, chirping, yelling, growling, all alive.
Yes, the silent place is there too.
I can't find my true self only on the mountain top;
I must descend and be among the living
And leave behind the perfect rocks,
Or pretend that I've become one of them.
In the noises of this world, I will find the Silence of my soul.
I shall continue walking.

❧ THE GIVER ❧

• I know now why I love you so much;
There's a piece of Me within you.
I have given you My smile,
And with My gaze, and My embrace, a gift that is yours to keep,
It comes first through Me
Then into you.
No wonder I love you so much! •
So you see, sweet brother, The One that gave it to me
Is going around like a honey bee
Collecting the pollen of my life
And making honey with His Love.

❧ SACRED PEBBLES ❧

I remember now,
Three pebbles lined up in perfect order, perfect order.
So perfect, see?
You came along has You do, and ready, always being there, ready,
And then You threw them away!
•There, go find them• you said, and so I go.
Then with a smile, You caressed my face and disappeared;
I have the largest collection of pebbles now, everywhere.
You seemed to be in each and every one of them.
In fact I know You are.

❧ MEETING THE MAKER ❧

Today I forgot the Divine One's existence,
I dressed myself in a thousand masks,
And I dove into an ocean of make believe
I died a false death,
I dried internal tears with bravado looks,
I faked a thunder under a fawn prayer,
I took refuge in the lie because my love got misplaced into an unknown
distant presence within my own,
Then you came sweet brother,
And I risked opening my sacred heart to your divine wisdom,
And you reminded me of my own words of hope and perseverance ,
You reminded me of the beauty of my simple humanness,
You shared with me the story of the man that wanted to be with God,
And how the angel offered him the path of suffering,
And there You were my Beloved ,
My masks fall to dust in the mystery of Your many loving faces I'm
humbled.
Again I'm in love.

❦ BREATHING ❧

I receive the golden light
I say yes
To the burden and the smile
I say yes
To the freedom and the pain
I say yes
To the brave and the coward
I say yes
To the embrace and the letting go
I say yes
As night arrives I say thank you for the day
As day emerges I say thank you for the night
With every and each breath
I say yes

❦ MUSE ❧

In the not so distant land of inspiration,
In the land of in the spirit,
The living mother muse abounds within,
Birth of fire
Birth of wind
Birth of earth
And of water therein,
In her bosom the nourishment of soul,
In her embrace the everlasting sweetness of courage, hope,
The ancient healing made present.
I become awake
Aware, and in my bow, the gentleness of being Her extension in my
words.
I listen, I thank, I write, I let go.

❧ THE SACRIFICE ❧

They both embraced and cried,

A cry like only two lovers can know,

One of willingness

One of separation

They both shared their tears in this invisible union of sorrow,

And time kept on as coolness took over but the memory remained.

Yes dear one, you are loved.

The light shines, that we know,

For the Father wills it into the heart of the ones that care.

And Healing is born.

❦ BEING NOTHINGNESS ❦

I am the light from which He shines,
I am the voice from which He speaks,
I am the smile from which He heals,
The hands from where the touch is eternal,
I am the presence of Him
That in thousands of millions of all that is,
Is a simple revelation of His beauty shared,
And I shall keep remembering that I am everything
In my humble nothingness.

❧ COMPASSION ❧

Very well then, sweet brother,
Sink your teeth into the sour grapes of my life,
Drink the spoiled milk of my misfortunes,
Bathe yourself in the muddy waters of my frustrations,
Pay my rent,
Pay my taxes,
Pay something,
Why the sudden silence?
Wait! where do you go?
Why the certain apathy
Where there was so much passion and certainty?
Are my moccasins too tight?
None of it has ever been needed, for my love for you transcends it all,
and you are welcome,
Leave the cloak of fear at the door, for in here your presence is one with
the Great Mystery.
Just Be.

❧ ALLOWING ❧

Allow, Allow, Allow, sweet brother,
Fret not over much doing,
For one may lose the beauty of the In breath,
Or the relief of the Out breath.
There, where the Unnamable resides,
The temple of all things known and unknown,
Will you persist in the questioning of the thousands of reasons The
river flows into his own whereabouts
Without minding us whatsoever?
Allow it.
May the woman at the well satisfy your thirst as she did to the Master,
May your flight be that of an eagle that has spared a dove.
Let time be a word written on seashore.
And may you die to yourself with great love and dignity,
For I'm already proud of you, and I do not matter a bit.

❧ WILLINGNESS ❧

You come to a fork in the road,

Take it, sweet brother,

Consider the generous question,

-Am I willing to take all that comes with it?

The Beloved shall be on either side, I can assure you,

In one He shall be your witness,

In the other the warm loving arms that will carry you to bliss.

Either one, Take it, sweet brother, it's your road after all.

❧ PONDER ❧

Ask the rabbit to kiss the serpent, and the very least you'll get is a silent look of disdain as he runs off.

Ask the serpent to kiss the rabbit, and be ready to ask yourself how much longer will you last before the poison takes over your every cell and sense.

❧ THE JUDGE ❧

Judge not where my foot as landed just now, sweet brother,
For your eyes have distanced themselves from your path.
Consider remaining focused on your trudging,
Lest your mind trick you into an abyss,
My prayer shall evoke gentler falls.

☙ MOTH ☙

Courteous sun, for how many blessings shall I keep thanking you?
And as for your lover the moon,
How many prayers shall I chant?
And how humble my heart gets, when you both bow to me
And lead to the One that shines through you,
Blind me again with that Divine Light,
I am the moth seeking the candle to happily die in Her Flame.

❧ JESUS ❧

I sat near this old man,
He quietly molded clay under his rough hands,
-What's your name sir, I asked.
-Jesus. He softly replied.
-Jesus the Christ? I asked.
-That would be me indeed my son.
He smiled and continued shaping and molding the clay.
I smiled back, I understood.

❧ SOME PATH ❧

Oh sweet grains of salt,

How ever so timely you added taste to my life,

When I fell for the conquest of yet another experience,

And became lost in the world.

How sweet is the taste of desperation,

For Christ lives in the very end of each breath,

If only I pay attention.

Golden jewels and shining diamonds may bless many other seekers.

For I now bow to the fallen leaves of life;

I shall continue to drink from that Well the good book speaks of.

❦ Unity ❦

The good saint warned me of the dark night of the soul,

The sweet mother blessed me with no greater love,

I was reborn in the divine magic of the union with the unseen,

In my heart I wrote prayers of solace,

In my spirit I blew winds of grace,

In my death I awoke in fire,

And man became one with the Beloved.

❧ NIGHT ☙

Night, Night, Night.
Will I truly recognize your full darkness once I arrive,
Will you continue to lure me with swift dreams of light,
With tender promises of rest, and gentleness of solitude,
Will I recognize Medusa in your overtones of seduction,
And forget my sandals at your door while reaching for a deeper ocean,
And the moon, yes your greatest sister,
The one that unveils your lies,
Would you be able to feign her attention while I take that last breath
and you shut all my windows?
Or will she denounce you to Christ himself while the sun will free me
from your shackles
And I wonder if bees shall seek the nectar of the blessed flowers.
You know, the ones that I will place in your remembrance.

❧ THE THIEF ❧

You came into the night, and knife in hand, you robbed me of all my belongings,
Thank You sweet brother,
But please wait, don't leave so fast,
Carve my chest and in there you can steal my precious treasure,
All yours to have, for I don't want to rob you of my most expensive possession,
Go on happy sweet brother, so that you may have the very essence of the Father of Light.

❧ TREASURE ❧

The existence of the man,
The man seeking the man,
The man finding the man
And losing himself in himself.
The existence of the Father Mother of Light
The man seeking the Glorious Unseen
The man finding it
And losing himself to it All
Oh, precious death, my Fire cannot be contained.

❦ RICHNESS ❧

Cardamom and turmeric all yours to have, if that's what you want,

Lilies and tulips - even the most rare too,

All that is delicately expensive,

And the perfume of your gods,

Line them all up in your grave,

I'll admire your persistence for I too once craved,

No, I'm no more awake than you, sweet brother, no more awake than you,

As for myself I pray for the stillness of this stone.

❧ GRASPING ❧

Grasp a hand of nothing,
And be content,
For in it you shall find the infinite happiness you continuously sought
in everything,
Like the foam into the shore
And the last whisper of a breath
You shall arrive to heaven sweet brother,
Yes nirvana is yours in that hand of nothingness.
No need to reach for another.

❦ SACRED HEART ❦

The red sounds of my drummer, beat further, and further,

The waters of Atlantis have opened,

The bells of Samsara rest,

The rooster has silenced his courage,

My drums beat harder,

The Presence is felt,

I am still,

The blood of heavens dried upon my lips,

I burst into a crying laughter, a foolish dance, a childish prayer,

The Presence is, it just is.

I too surrender now.

This Sacred Heart keeps on beating.

❦ THE MEETING ❧

I heard a laughter in the dark,
I looked,
There on his knees sat my sweet brother yelling in tears of joy,
Cries of madness,
Laughing thunder in meekness,
Hands clasped to his chest, he hailed:
•I've found Him, I've found Him, I've found Him…
God has been hiding in here all these years, I've found him•
I wiped my own tears, I bowed and rejoiced.

❦ HOLY LONGING ❦

I know the voice of the wilderness,

And I know the voice of bewilderment,

That cry of longing,

Where trails of sorrow are left incomplete,

Where paths of wisdom are still submerged in dark veils of unknown,

The holy longing, the Holy One,

Tears distilled to diamonds,

The eternal searching for this Unseen Love that keeps on giving.

My River shall not run dry.

❧ OMEGA ❧

The north winds came to leave you a message,
A message already known by you, right?
Yes, that all that is, it isn't,
That all that became, was gone,
The snake shed her skin,
The cell renews,
The phoenix rises every so often,
And we forget. No harm in that,
For even the forgetfulness gets reminded of the noble truth,
All that is born shall perish,
All that shines shall dull,
After the darkness the light,
Listen till the end of the message, sweet brother,
For the good news is that in the emptiness of it all,
We shall remain forever alive in the Breath of the Beloved.
The Great I Am, where all that remains and is, really is His.
Everlasting Love and Wisdom.

❧ Mirror ❧

So it is, we cross paths
Yes, those are the branches of my tree of life,
You say they are bare and loveless,
Shadow no soul and warm no being,
Feed no sentient, nourish no element,
Purposeless, you said.
No, sweet brother, it wasn't me that lifted the mirror
Into your loving face.

❧ TRUDGING ❧

What a treasure I've not found,
What richness I'm blessed with - the unseen gems,
Gems of glory and superior wealth,
Like nothing in this world
What treasure I've not found
What Treasure I gained in my seeking,
I'm humbled.

❧ Beloved ❧

I'll never see Your precious full face in here,

I'll keep on seeking,

For I'll recognize Your eyes in my sweet brother,

And Your words in the longing of the winds,

Your healing in the drops of rain,

Your presence in the cry of the eagle,

I'll drink Your milk from the Mother of Truth,

And I'll eat Your sustenance from the Mother of Care,

And perfume my body with the fragrance of Your amber candles,

I know, I know I'm but a lunatic of a man that still holds petals of love

from his hands to his lips,

I'll keep on seeking

I'll keep on seeking

Your face is everywhere

My blindness continues to heal

Maybe not here, but there where the angels bathe in honey milk I shall

than see Your full face,

Fall to my knees and be satisfied in Your Magnificence,

I bow

I bow, to You I bow

❦ THE SONG ❦

You chanted, You chanted, You chanted,

Oh my Sweet One, my heart is radiating with the love in Your voice.

Blessings, blessings, blessings,

Abound within me with the hour of awakening, and whirl me within

Your Song,

I'm Yours, I'm Yours, I'm Yours

What Kindred Spirit has visited me?

An angel indeed,

Sing, chant, and be within me Oh Sweet Beloved.

❧ SHARING ❧

So the fire consumed you,
Good, share your flame with me, sweet brother,
Melt the ice within my forgetfulness,
Warm the place of my horizon,
Light the way of my wonders,
And be a flame with the sacredness of my heart,
For fire shared, is love laced in forgiveness,
And I shall continue to bow to your generosity.

❧ SELF LOVE ❧

So yes, here we are speaking of reunion,

Yes, I'm am the Rock on which you rest your tired body,

Yes, I'm the Air that restores your senses,

Yes, I'm the Food that graces your soul and allows the smile to emerge
upon your lips

Yes, in that mirror you contemplate Me,

And Yes, you are loving no more than yourself.

How glad I am of your return!

❧ Revisit ❧

I came back to the original visit.

Mind you, I didn't go back.

You can't ever go back.

But the visit can be done again and again

And as a silver drop of morning dew,

The ocean awaits the beloved reconnection.

I'm back home, for the first time.

Oh Precious Silence of the Eternal Infinite,

My last breath was left among Your dream of my existence,

And it was good.

I, too, belong, as I always did, in the most promising future of being.

❦ FALLEN ❦

Yes, I have fallen,
Yes, again,
My knees are scraped, my hands are bloodied, my face is a disgrace,
My body is wrecked, my emotions are shredded, my spirit ...
My spirit just got up again
Yes, I am standing up.

❦ THIRST ❧

Forgive me, sweet brother, for I cannot quench your thirst,
As you cannot quench mine;
Waters may flow over us and even drown us,
But the thirst we are afflicted with can only be satisfied by Fire,
Shalom, Shalom, Shalom

❧ THE BEAST WITHIN ❧

In the forest of my soul, there lives a wild beast,
Untamed, and vicious, dangerous and dark,
No plea to be made,
No reason to be reckoned,
Only love will kill him,
Only life will bring him to life.

❧ Peace ❧

My sweet brother looked at me and said:
• Teach me about your peace.•
-Yes, sweet brother, I shall:
My heart is heavy with longing,
My mind is troubled with judgment,
My words are empty in anger,
My actions are lost with envy,
My relationships are tormented with my existence,
And to all of it I've said - Yes
And I've bowed to my imperfections.
Here's my peace.

❧ THE CALLING ❧

Something is calling my name,
I hear it,
Sometimes closer, some other times far away,
A gentle call,
A gentle whisper,
I know it as the Holy Longing,
My heart bleeds for it.
My mind is no longer mine,
The awaiting is torturous,
I crave the sweetness of my Beloved.
I breathe again.

❦ MEDITATION ❧

Only this breath is real,
Only this breath is real,
Only this breath is real,
The shadows that consume me, a lie.
The voices that torment me, a lie.
The sounds that torture me, a lie.
The emotions that contort me, a lie.
The thoughts that blind me, a lie.
I'm tired,
I'm tired.
I pray for courage, I pray for another breath
Lord of Life, hear my plea,
Take this breath of mine, and make it my last one, that I may again be
reunited in Your Holy Love.

❧ THE QUESTION ❧

And the self asked:

-Who are you to attempt to speak so eloquently about the Father of
Light?

- I am no one,

Only a fool that felt the burning of the Wisdom of Love,

And now I run in circles seeking the hidden face of Him that kissed me
in my desperation.

❧ LOVE ❦

What waters shall wash away the inside of this body?
None, none whatsoever.
It is bloody and inflamed, dark and muggy.
Bring the Fire of God to purify this foolish man,
Let me die in His Eternal Flame.

❧ SILENCE ❧

In mirages of hopelessness I built a fortress of loneliness,
I built a castle of sorrow,
A harem of lies,
And my sweet brother knocked,
I refused to answer.
The walls grew thicker and the vastness of desperation laced every bre-
ath,
But how bitter sweet is the gift of abandonment
And the peculiar way of dying to all that was!
For the Kiss of Seasons blessed me,
And the Sunlight of the Spirit floored me in the very essence of Love.
And He, the One, whispered loud into my soul,
•Welcome home, son, your 40 days in the desert are over.•
I finally tasted the Fire, and it was good,
For my sweet brother finally broke bread with me.
And I exhale.

❧ HUMANNESS ❧

Not trying, but dying, sweet brother,

Here I lay my life at the feet of the Almighty so that He may slay me,

I've known the passions and desires,

The flesh and the greed,

I've known it all,

And in all I came out alive, and suffering,

And I wanted more, until more became unbearable,

I could no longer breathe,

So I died, and died again, and shall continue dying for as long as the

Beloved may let me,

I die in Him, for Him, and I gain all that is life,

And I breathe, again, and again.

❧ THE GIFT ❧

You asked me for a plate of food, I gave You my meal.
You asked for a cup of water,
I gave You my well.
You asked me for a breath,
I gave You my life.
You gave me Your Love
You gave me Your Love
You gave me Your Love.

❦ HEALING ❧

Slay me in water,
Slay me in fire,
Slay me in spirit,
I bow to Your willingness to slay me.
My temple pours out the cries of time,
You recognize my tears,
You dry my face with Your Divine Wind.
So slay me with Your Elements,
Let my death be a demonstration of Your Eternal Love,
Let my Life be as it may be, a healing balm
To my sweet brother, to my sweet sister.

✄ SIGHT ✄

Trust not on the seen, fellow traveler,
For you might be shortsighted, even blinded.
The seen shall eventually turn to ashes,
Like you and me.
Melt ever so gently into the Unseen, sweet brother,
The Gold that never melts,
The Fire that is never extinguished,
The Love that will never leave you.

❧ DESTINY ❧

In the canoe of insecurity I sailed over here,

On the wings of uncertainty I flew over there,

In the torso of longing I returned again,

And again, in the winds of fantasy I departed,

And so it is that in the end of my breath I come back,

In the end of the night the sun emerges,

My body dies again and again.

I shall return,

And He remains.

❦ GOD'S HOME ❦

There's a place where God hides His face,
I look around and cannot find,
So I look for a replacement,
I crawl then in agony,
In scars, turmoil, and confusion,
To find again His ecstasy,
And understand that all this loss has been an illusion,
He never left, walked away, fell apart,
The Beloved hid His face in the center of my heart,
So when man tells me that the almighty is in a building,
Or in a place out there, somewhere in space
I smile and say yes there's a place,
The building, a temple,
The temple, inside,
Where the Spirit lives,
Where my God Hide

❦ BEST FRIEND ❧

Embrace kindness, sweet brother,

Let the rains of anger become water

Flowing through your fingertips,

So that the stronghold of fear shall not grip you.

Recognize the shining light within you,

For within your heart center

Lies the temple of the Divine,

Consider visiting it quite often,

Allowing a smile upon your lips so that your mind may follow it,

Be aware, sweet brother, that your mind is but a servant of your heart,

That your heart is the gentle power force of your inner beauty,

Cater to him.

You'll meet the One that will bring the greatest ecstasy, healing, joy,

serenity, into your life,

That someone is You.

❧ MEETING ME ❧

Yes, silence me,
Silence me silence me
For in my silence I shall meet the one I must reckon with,
The one that carves the heart with judgment and strips away compas-
sion,
The one that dries the heart of joy and poisons it with pride,
The one that invents lies in place of honesty,
I shall meet with him,
And I shall love him until love gains some other name,
I shall nourish him until his tears become sighs,
I shall comfort him until he lays himself on my lap in rest,
For I will be laying myself in the lap of the Almighty.

❦ Sweetness of Christ ❦

How can I explain the color of milk to my blind brother?
How can I explain the sweetness of Christ to the all-knowing wise
man?
I am a foolish, simple man, who has no knowledge whatsoever of
divine things,
Blind myself, I can only offer the taste of the sweet milk,
And say, Yes God is there too.

❧ ETERNAL LOVER ❧

Said it in color,
Said it in sound,
In crushing blows all around,
In magic moments, in times of bliss,
In crying torments, in times like this,
Said it again, said it over and over.
He loves forever,
My God, my Beloved, Eternal Lover.

❧ Broken Cup ☙

Yes, I see the broken cup,

Do I see it's uselessness and ridicule?

How can I?

For I am the cup that has fallen and been broken,

And the Creator is gluing my pieces with His eternal Love,

I'll pick up the pieces,

And I'll offer them to the Father of Light,

Now. . . .will you?

❦ CLAY ❦

Here is my nakedness,
All my frailties and my vulnerabilities,
I am the cup for Your wine,
Pour it within me,
I am the clay for Your hands,
The pen for Your hands,
Your poem to be written,
Scribble in me Sweet Lord,
Mold me into Your perfection,
May my blood be fire in your will,
My madness, Your eternal truth,
Kill the liar within me,
May my strange nakedness be Your gentle revelation,
My shortcomings Your way to my surrenders,
My loud cry, the morning bell of Your wakefulness.

❧ THUNDER ❧

Drums of thunder, sounds of Might,

Rivers of soul into the night,

Calling of Wonder,

Tears of Light,

Healing in sight…

Healing in sight.

❧ BECOMING ❧

I become the drop in the ocean and the ocean in the drop
The grain of sand in the desert and the desert in the grain of sand
The wind and the waves
The forest and the mountain
The tree and the grass blade
I become the ant and the buffalo
The sparrow and the eagle
The serpent and the mouse
The ray of light, of hope
The streaming flow of joy
The sound, and the silence
The poem, and the pen
The voice, and the song
The wine into water
The man into child
The child into God
I become the Great I Am
Into the lovingness of my nothingness.

❧ WINDOWS ❧

What windows do you speak of, fellow traveler?

There's this one where you can see my soul, and all is light,

And there's this one where you see my thoughts, and you must run for shelter,

And then this one where you shall embrace me as yourself

And a living kiss shall wash us with the milk of forgiveness.

Be willing to look, my dear one.

❧ THE PRAYER ❧

There I lay my prayers,

In winds of mortar and castles of sand,

I fall back into the cradle of the Almighty,

And there's still no sweeter death.

The lies that once created the tapestry of this false self,

Are now memories of deep wounds, slashes of desperation, Brought to

my knees in the presence of the Eternal Truth.

Once I built a dream, it was a seed,

I forgot to ask the Sweet Presence to water it for me,

His promise remains:

That I shall be loved despite the imposed adage of fantasy.

In stone stairways I climb now,

His fire burning me from the inside out,

I lay my prayers above my head,

The temple inside insists,

I fall back again,

Now I know.

❦ NOURISHMENT ❦

On the wings of a dove, I let my soul travel to find the never-ending
longing for my Beloved.
I drank from the rivers of fire,
Rivers that died in oceans and became currents of love,
I ate from the land where I bury my sorrows,
And nourished my soul from the fruits of my desperation.
I met the face of my Beloved in the tears
Reflected in the mirror as I turn my back away from Him,
On the wings of darkness, I flew into the Light.
I now wash myself in flights of tenderness,
Dry myself in the waters of compassion,
And let my ashes be spread over the sands of His gentle embrace,
I'm home.
On wings of hope I fly into the Blessed Essence,
My sacred heart right open, all sorrows and lost dreams exposed.
I am a sparrow of Light, a child in the Mother's bosom,
The scars are made new,
I am reborn in the cradle of my Beloved arms.

❧ SMOKY MIRROR ❧

Once deciding to allow the bitterness inside to remain,
The man walks into the depth of his own loss,
Eyes closed to the light and the Beloved inside,
He walks close to the fake mirror that speaks the false images he belie-
ves he wants to see,
The calling gets shut in the morning tiredness,
And the night falls as a false fire of relief,
The Beloved has begun to cry, and man pretends He's not there.

❦ EGO ❦

Am I just a bag of broken bones?
Or just an empty vessel of empty spirit?
Will You embrace this darkness?
This imperfect fool?
This runaway infant where dreams got stolen and then were turned
into a lie by his own self?
Will You cradle the head of this liar, thief, absorbed in the essence of
his non-existence?
Are the gifts of my own humanness a layout of shards of castaway cold
ceramic,
Where even the colors refuse to get close to each other?
And the tapestry of delusion sits inward in rotten waters of illness
The ridicule of self-importance.

❦ DARK VEIL ❦

My words got stolen as if a dark veil of a forgotten canyon imploded
from without,
The fire has been hidden in the crevices of dawn,
The crying of the Muse is heard within my distant heart beat,
I crave Him, I seek Him, in all the turns and twists of desperation and
waves of framing thoughts,
Left almost behind, this spirit of mine remains resilient,
For I have tasted the sweetness of the Fire,
My sacred heart longs,
I cry,
I'm empty, without Him, I'm empty.

❧ MORNING PRAYER ❧

In solitude I seek refuge in Your Sacred Heart O My Creator,

Not that I isolate from my fellow man,

But that in You, in Your silence,

I may become a better servant to my brother,

In whatever humble form that might be.

Let me then become the grass blade,

The grain of sand,

The unheard song,

Your hidden breath

That I may die in You daily,

Amen.

❦ THE CRY ❧

There's no ego in this breath of mine
The body pain transcends the thought
The emotional suffering holds to the heart as leeches
My blood is drained
The solitude is questioning herself
My voice is just too tired to even try to be heard
I breathe, I don't even want to
But I do, and I know that I am with the Father.
How dark it is before the dawn, indeed!

❦ Exhaling ❧

Have I become my last breath?
If so, why the loving pushing into my lungs of your Divine air?
You simply refuse to let me go,
Your Love abounds in every single breath of mine,
I may gaze away in selfishness,
But you compassionately place yourself in me at every moment,
And the whisper,
O how can I ignore that whisper that continuously warms me ...
•Be still, my child, be still and know that I Am•
I inhale.

❦ BREATH OF FIRE ❦

Embracing the Light one breath at a time,
Renewing the Love one moment at a time,
I am the flame in the Eternal Fire,
I burn in Love,
I burn in Eternity,
The child of the Most High, I am.
In sweet wine of faith, I become,
To all that is, I die,
For the Unseen has arrived in my door,
And in my heart has made residence,
So I breathe,
The breath of Fire I breathe.

❧ DESIRE ❧

What is the color of desire?

Would it be the same as the eagle cry?

Or the unfolding of a long night?

Can it be the silence of a mother's tear?

The hiding nakedness of the shy lover?

Or the cutting of a sudden faith?

Could it be the prayer that was unanswered?

Or the word that went unspoken?

What of the murmur of ecstasy just left by the memory of a fleeting
dream?

The blood of the beloved?

The burning fire of becoming?

Will desire allow a color to be a color?

Will it remain it's own?

❦ GRATITUDE ❦

Another night,
Another day of surrender,
The lost falls,
And the internal gazes are now to display on this solemn path
The unconscious one,
Where I obey to the freedom of being naked, alive, truth to self.
Let me then die to this joyful living,
For tomorrow I'll awake.

❧ THE WISE ONE ❧

It's so much more than surrender,
Yes, I know you know that.
It's much more than willingness,
Yes, I know you know that.
It's much more than faith,
Yes, I know you know that.
In fact, I know you know all of it,
How sad that you refuse to know yourself.
How sad that you fear your own salvation
And will not walk into the fire.

❧ FACE TO FACE ❧

The virtue Heavenly Father?

My faith? My seemingly good deeds? Even my willingness?

I dare to renounce it as lies of my humanness,

For as I gaze into the colorful lily, her demands are none,

Her beauty abounds freely, in love, in eternal service.

What about the sparrow and his hymn to You, while he praises You in eloquent melodies;

I steal the sounds, and in that he rejoices too.

And the grass under my feet, how I crush the beauty of their blades - completely blind to their existence,

Only to be welcomed later on the same path with the same surrender.

And the trees, the waters, the air I breathe, O Father of Light, will I ever redeem my inadequacy?

I'm poor in spirit, but arrogant in thought,

Poor in faith, grandiose in presence,

Poor in knowledge, and abuse Your name to elevate myself above my brothers and sisters.

What virtue will ever come out of such hypocrisy???

I beg Your Forgiveness and, in fear, Your Compassion as well.

❦ Suffering ❦

The beast is hungry my Lord,
The beast is angry my Lord,
The beast is screaming for more, More, MORE
I'm not enough, but I'm better than them,
Should I move like this, is this way okay,
Are my words proper, is my look slender,
Am I convincing them,
Am I lying to myself,
O the beast is awake my Lord,
And is reflecting my image
In the sedentary waters of my own suffering.

❧ BELOVED MUSE ❧

In You I repose my Muse,

In You I rest and let Your Divine cradle rock me into sleep,

How sweet is this death,

This death of unknowing, and knowing all that You are, is real, my Muse.

And what form will it take,

Does not matter; I'm already there and the ecstasy shall remain,

I repose in You my Beloved Creator,

I die in You, I'm dead to everything else,

I'm Your fool in the rain,

Your drunkard of poppy fields,

Your baby of innocence,

The fragrant incense in my view

Will be just a gentle remembrance of You, my Muse.

❦ THE THIEF ❧

Your thief, Your thief, Your thief I am, my Lord.

I steal the breath of Self from every existential moment and lay it at

Your feet,

In my thoughts,

In my prayers,

In my laments,

In my rejoicing,

In contemplation,

In Your silence I steal Your sweetness,

I bathe in Your fragrance,

I beg Your forgiveness.

❧ BECOMING LOVE ❧

That summer afternoon, I laid my head on your lap under that olive
tree,
There I surrendered to becoming the stone on which You chiseled me
to Your likeness,
There I surrendered to becoming the clay to which You molded me to
Your essence,
There I surrendered to becoming the child in which Your love has Your
existence,
And from Your bosom I tasted the honey suck milk of life,
The caring breeze of Your breath as my own,
The touch that let it me know I'm enough,
In fact in You I became everything - that is Love.

❦ VEILS ❦

Veils of night,
Your vain attempts to hide my Beloved
Are lost in the mere mention of His name.
You may blind my eyes,
You may cover my body,
You shall not hinder my heart,
And there's where He lives.

❦ PRAISE ❧

It was the last waving of the condor's wing,

Or perhaps the last whisper of the Sahara wind.

I don't know, I do know that my tears washed me closer to You,

And that my broken soul mended faster as You traveled through.

That the island that was me became the grain of sand on shore that You walked upon.

But it was Your scented perfume, my Lord, that awoke me to Your eternity,

Please, let my death in this ongoing moment be only for You,

Worshiping Your Merciful Light with all my senses,

Thank You, O magnificent Condor,

Thank You, majestic wind of the eternal Sahara,

My blessing lies in Your gift of awareness,

Shalom Shalom Shalom

ℰ CLOSING TIME ℛ

A warrior awoke yesterday,

Blade in hand, siege in heart.

A storm arose yesterday,

Blinding sand, split apart.

The Lover cried yesterday,

Tears on end, longing shall part.

The knight lost his armor,

The dragon, his breath,

The whale, her song,

Life, her death,

The hand of the Merciful glided over the forest shadows,

Returned to the Meadows,

The only trees remaining, Willows.

And the fountain will flame,

Fires refrain,

The moment is here,

Eternity, now.

We all shall sleep well tonight.

❦ PASSOVER ❧

What generous table You set before me!
How full is my cup!
Me, who meant to be Your server, am now the blessed son,
Your Loving Mercy knows no bounds,
Even the bitter herbs have sweetest taste,
Thank You, Thank You, Thank You.

❦ COMING HOME ❧

I touched the garment that healed me,
I was covered by the veil of light,
And the veil of darkness vanished,
I dance and swirl,
I cry and laugh,
The Almighty is leading me home,
I have begun to recognize my own Self.

❦ DIVINE MAGIC ❧

Can I consider divine magic?
What of the piercing of heart?
And the boundless waves of nothingness?
The cries of the deep?
And the screaming of silence?
All divine?
I must answer yes,
For I have stumbled into the knowing of the stepping stone…
Into the bliss of grace.

❦ SUPPLICATION ❧

Who allowed the night to fall upon my morning,

Surely I did!

But how could I have slipped into the veils of suffering if I was wide

awake?

O Lord hear my supplication,

I have lied to myself and have believed my own words,

I run to nothing, speaking of You,

I embellish my stars, when it is darkness that accompanies me,

I wish Your Presence, but have locked the door between us,

How shall You reach me if I can't even recognize my own soul,

How I so want Your saving!

❧ LOST ❧

My cup has dried.
My horizon has dwindled.
I fall into the bottomless abyss of illusion.
I don't know where north is.
I can't recall the garden.
I remain to pray that silence shall heal this fool.

❧ SPARROW ❧

Moment by moment,
The opportunity to say yes to life,
For the Light is eminent in my heart,
As gratitude bows me to my knees in adoration of You, my Lord.
Just the knowing of being a sparrow in Your Infinity,
I bow, I bow, I bow.

❦ GIFT OF DESPERATION ❧

How sweet You are, You Gift of Desperation,
That You turn my tears into diamonds,
My loneliness into solitude,
My struggles into blessings,
I hold You in high esteem my Dear,
For in You I have walked the paved way to the Divine Presence.
I surrender.

❦ THE SHADES OF THE SHADOW ❧

I walk into the fire, yes I have become a eternal flame,

I have jumped into the ocean , yes I have eternally drowned,

I die again, in the fire and in the ocean of your Majestic Mercy.

I have known Self,

And all that has been is a lie of shades of the shadow,

Waves of illusion, where Your will has been pulled back,

And ego propelled as tides,

Indeed I have drowned in the strange ocean of myself ,

And created volcanoes of misery,

But what sweet surrender, that of desperation,

O my Merciful Lord, my blood has become your flames ,

My heart, Your furnace,

My years, Your rivers,

My soul, Your ocean where my death brings me to Life.

❧ GIFT OF LIFE ❧

What gratitude for each breath!
You live in every inhale,
You free me in every exhale,
The origins of You bless me at every moment,
What words can express my thankfulness?
None.
So I bow, and again, I breathe,
And in the very silence of all,
You receive my naked appreciation with Your Gift of Life.

❧ Thank You ❧

Thank You, Thank You, Thank You,
Thank You for all that I am and for all that I am not,
Thank You for all that I was and for all that I was not,
Thank You for all the I will be and for all that I will not,
In You I am everything ,
Alone I am not.

❦ GARDENS OF PRESENT ❧

Gardens of my present,
Arch of my past,
Tides of my future,
I'm drunk in the Divine Wine of the Almighty,
For in the Alpha and Omega,
I die and am reborn again and again,
The Arch of the past holds wisdom,
The Tides of the future, all the hopes and dreams,
In the Gardens of the present
I allow my sober drunkenness to be everlasting,
I drink from Him who showers my soul with Love,
I am eternal.

❧ THE ROSE ☙

Which Rose, with which color, shall reveal the wisdom of time?

Will I return to the divine land?

Will my dust be left untouched?

The walk into the many things unseen,

Were they sways of longing from You, Great Spirit?

The Rose will unfold, She will reveal;

Leave your bothersome questions for yesterdays,

For today you live in here, right now,

And the Rose shall remain a Rose.

❦ THE SUN ❦

So it is that the Sun remains bright regardless of the clouds of life,
The hot rays of Truth shall continue to pierce darkness in the most
loving way,
When He shines He makes no distinctions,
Shining on all that is beauty because all is beauty,
My redeeming heart pretended ignorance,
But the surrender is sublime.
The light shall shine always,
Why not bathe in the Sun,
Keep the faith in the Sun,
Keep the faith in the Son.

❦ WAITING ON THE LORD ❧

May the ground disappear beneath my feet,
And the winds blow my shelter,
May the oceans take my life,
May the fires consume my soul,
It is You, my Lord, calling my name,
In You, my Lord I shall be held in Love,
Being born again as I take my last breath.
Shalom Shalom Shalom

❦ THANKS GIVING ❦

Yes, drink from this fountain.

As I drink with you,

For our thirst now and always shall be quenched,

My brother, the sweet coyote, had a gentle way of smiling at me the

other night,

I almost became too important to say thank you, but I did.

And the tree that sheltered me from the hot sun today whispered, In

waves of silence, that my head was getting taller

I almost forgot to bow, but I did.

And the sparrow that awoke me this morning cried a hymn for my lost

will,

I almost forgot to call on my spirit in him, but I did.

What gratitude!

So I say unto you, fellow traveler,

Drink, drink from this fountain,

I did remember to offer my silence for the grateful blessing.

❦ MADNESS ❧

Roll, Roll, Roll, sweet brother,
Let the ecstasy of your movement bring you a little closer,
Swirl, swirl, swirl, mad man,
You are there, and all the rest of them remain blind,
With each drop of sweat the divine juice is present,
On the floor up above, sing your praises to the Fire of Eternity,
O how your adoration is no less than a dance,
It is the very life blood in the veins of us!
Jump in the fire now, you maniacs,
I shall tear my garments and follow you, for now I see.

❧ THE TASTE OF FORGIVENESS ❧

Sweet honey taste of forgiveness,
The balm of the heavens poured upon me as honey milk,
I embrace the child,
I kiss the spirit,
I returned to the rebirth moment of innocence,
The space between is safe,
The loving distance heals the wound,
I recognize my own offenses,
And the path is now clear,
The veil of injury has fallen,
I offer myself to You, Father of Light.

❧ WATERS OF LOVE ❧

Is this pool of blood as clear as the waters of love?

Yes, I hear...

The bleeding is from the heart,

The love flow is from the heart,

Lord you speak to me from the heart, so I rejoice in my injuries,

As in my joys,

And perhaps I still cry in my humanness,

I shall see those tears as Your loving healing flowing through me,

After all, You are all that is, all that is Love, because You love,

I shall continue to love You, and in all that is,

I shall remain in love,

In blood, wind, tears, rain, smiles, mountains, silence, rivers, waters, in waters of love...

❦ SURRENDERING ❧

I surrender, yes I surrender,
That my laughter be a invitation to you,
I surrender,
That my tears be a safe welcome to yours,
I surrender,
That my walk invite you,
I surrender,
That in my stillness I become you,
I surrender,
For the Almighty has offered me a brother and a sister,
That I see myself so I can lose myself and find Him.
O Lord, to You I surrender.

❦ ONENESS ❦

Christ, Christ, Christ, Christ,

Buddha, Buddha, Buddha, Buddha,

Great White Spirit, Great White Spirit, Great White Spirit, Great White
Spirit.

Allah, Allah, Allah, Allah,

Krishna, Krishna, Krishna, Krishna

Jehovah, Jehovah, Jehovah, Jehovah,

All of You Divine Beloveds of Oneness,

Quench my thirst for my fountain is dried,

I beg of you for lonely is my path if made out of self,

And my own blindness may injure me forevermore,

And I fear not recognizing any of you and myself.

Feed me the manna of your presence O Lord,

I'm hungry for your taste,

I crave your very essence,

I'm naked in my own illusion,

I'm bare in delusion,

All of you I beg,

Gently and I repeat gently bring me back home,

My cell has darkened,

My candle is loosing her thread.

❦ Sheltered ❦

In glorious morning I find You,
In gentle evenings I embrace You,
In the gardens of doubt You comfort me,
In the oceans of fear You assure me.
I'm the bird out of the nest,
The lamb on trial,
The voice of innocence,
Almighty, thank You for the shelter in Your mansion of hope,
Thank You for the guidance in Your trails of calm,
I breathe, I seek You
I breathe, I find You.
I breathe You.

❧ VOLCANO ❧

It surges as hot lava and no water seems to cool it,

As desert summers the torrential sand storms have gripped my loins,

I cry out to You, for the enemy continues to punish me,

I pray for Your deliverance, I pray for surrender, I do,

I wait, I trust,

So much love to be experienced, but the volcanoes of my humanness
roar through my gentle soul,

Father, Father, I beg Your forgiveness,

For the enemy is the writer of these words.

How can I love You so deeply and hate Your existence in all that is?

I'm baffled with my suffering,

But not unsure whatsoever of my Love for You.

❧ SEEKING THE BELOVED ☙

I bow to the offering of Your tears within my eyes,
I bow to the offering of Your suffering within my heart,
I bow to the offering of Your seeming absence within my mind,
That I may continue to seek You, my Lord, in all that is.
Amen.

❧ BLISS ❧

In the midst of these storms,
I shall remember Your calm,
Your loving quiet presence,
Your assuring whisper to my surrender,
And I shall return to the Garden of Love
And be a part of Your fragrant bliss.

❧ IN YOU ☙

In You I become the wind that caresses my face,

In You I become the remaining dust instead of my place,

In You I become the river that washes my feet,

In You I become the space in between where we meet,

In You I become the silence of life,

In You I become the nothingness of death that I strive,

In You I become the flame and the wave,

In You I become the sweetness I crave,

In You I become the darkness of crucifixion,

In You I become the light of resurrection,

In You I Am.

❧ ESSENCE ☙

This blood of mine,
Where the very essence of You remains,
And these eyes of mine, where the very soul of Yours reflects,
What words can be said?
None whatsoever,
Let my blood flow in ecstasy and my eyes see You, the Unseen.
And in my bleeding,
And in my crying,
I shall share in the suffering with you, my sisters and brothers,
I shall become a beacon of light and hope in the midst of sorrow.
I shall,
I Am.

❦ THE DREAM ❧

It's just a dream,

This dream of reality, unbelief,

The dense veil of life,

The trance of unreality,

The sleepwalking moment of the ordinary,

How great is the suffering of self

The illusion of the lie to which we succumb!

Let me die to your sweetness O my Creator,

Uncover my blinded eyes, my own lying,

In faith I shall find my own true being in You my Beloved,

So let the manifestation of the desire for humility and gratitude be
enough to please You,

That I may live in Your forever sweetness,

That my blood be Your honey,

My breath, Your life,

My heart, Your living place of Love, Life, and Healing towards all of
Your creatures.

❦ Seasons ❦

Let me be the winter in my summer,

Let me be the fall in my spring,

Let me be all of Your seasons, for You created me for being so,

How can I deny the blackness of the night and the beauty of her mystery,

Can one just gain pleasure from the morning sun while he lays?

All belongs.

I thank You.

❧ CANDLE ❧

Feminine me,

Masculine me,

Allow me to be Your wife,

Allow me to be Your husband,

Shape within me all the facets of this diamond of Yours,

That Your precious light may shine within me,

That I may be a light to the world,

Even in the form of a candle.

❧ FULLNESS OF LIFE ☙

Even the white rose petals cast shadows on themselves,
And doesn't the moon in all her magnificence allow her beauty to
reveal her darkness?
And so it is that the more the observer and the light present itself,
Embracing all that is, the unity of complete Self,
Turning shades of shame and fear into the Lightness of Divinity,
Blessings are present,
Perceiving them is the blessing.

❦ TREASURE ❦

For what seemed centuries I franticly looked everywhere,
Saw everything, found nothing.
Now with closed eyes and open heart, I find the eternal universe,
I find You, my Love, my God, my Christ.

❧ THE FEATHER ❧

It just fell,

That delicate little white feather just fell,

As if it were your eyes gently closing on my soul,

I stayed with it and smiled,

More than an embrace, more than a kiss, it was just your loving way of reminding me,

• I Am here, you know.•

Yes, I smiled.

❦ EMBRACING THE SHADOW ❦

Flee not from your shadow, sweet brother and sister,
For in it you shall find your surrender and forgiveness,
You'll discover the gold within yourself,
You'll transform yourself into the gifts of the Almighty Beloved.

❧ FLAMES ❧

Yes, I see the glorious sun,
And I surrender to the majesty of the moon,
But your light O Lord, my Beloved,
I ascend in flames in the mere thought of You.

❧ DISCOVER ❧

It was me again, My Beloved,
I lost myself in Your essence
Only to discover myself in You,
Only to discover Yourself in me,
I am Light, I AM.

❦ THE SUN AND THE MOON ❦

I look into the eyes of my perceived enemy,
I offer forgiveness.
I look into my own eyes,
I offer forgiveness.
I am the Sun and the Moon,
The light and the shadow,
The seen and unseen,
As I exhale I surrender.

❦ TRAVELER ❦

What a cry for righteousness!
Sweet brother, your face reddens,
And your heart beats fast.
Where have you misplaced the Living God?
O blessed humility of the gentle observer,
And the faithful prayer warrior,
May we trudge in the dust of their sandals.
For the mirror, the Divine Beloved is not hidden,
It surely abides in my eyes and in your eyes.
Feel how sickness strikes you, fellow traveler,
For anger and judgment manifested are the ways of the lost.
Please trust me, I recognize the path,
For like you, sweet one, I am a traveler too.

❦ WHYS ❦

Why so many questions...
Please allow...allow ...
Let lilies be lilies
And waterfalls, inspiration,
Remain an open heart,
With eyes of contemplation,
Forgive...forgive...forgive
Let your question become a Thank You
And you shall win the world.

❧ HIM BEING ME ❧

You asked me to look at the skin of my brother,
Please forgive me, for I'm blind to such things,
I do see a radiant beauty bursting out of his body.
You asked me to comment on the religion of my brother,
Please forgive me for I'm speechless to such things,
I do hear the sound of his divine creation.
You asked me to compare myself with my brother,
Please forgive me for I am ignorant to such things,
For when I look at him all I see is myself.

❦ CHILD OF GOD ❦

My eyes are shut, but I see so clear,

My heart, a volcano,

The top of my head, a lotus flower,

My growing, a river,

Throw me into the Essence of Your Existence,

Empty my being, for I can only become solace in Your presence,

I am all of these things,

With eyes open, I am just Your child.

❧ THE PATH ❧

I look, I seek, I continue.

The path is long, crooked, veiled;

I remain,

I look, sometimes I see You, sometimes I do not,

But I feel You.

I seek, and know that it pleases You, and I feel You

I continue, for I know that to stop is to die into darkness

And no longer feel You.

So I trudge.

❦ DELIVERANCE ❧

Do not hide Your sweet face from me, O Lord,
For all laziness will possess me
And the lies will take me saying, "You are but a lost mist in a distant truth."
I hurt, I am falling, maybe my high expectations of You are just that,
Please prove my enormous ego wrong,
And deliver me from doubt.

❧ HUMBLENESS ☙

I've been in this position before,
I believe everyday,
On my knees I humble myself to your Love,
So I can be that Love,
That I can bow to the foam of the shore,
To the grain of sand,
To the ant, and the beetle, the snake, and the sparrow, the eagle and the
buffalo, I bow,
To the lily and the rosemary, the oak and the olive tree I bow,
To my neighbor, I bow,
That to him I can be You.

❦ HEART SHINING ❦

The night brings the darkness,
But the stars are forever present,
My sacred heart shines brighter than the moon,
Gently guiding my way towards You,
And I find You again, and again
In that sane place that others see shining from within me.
How grateful I am to You, my Beloved Christ.

❧ EMPTINESS ❧

Oh how I empty myself,
So that I may know myself,
So that I may know my brother,
So that I forgive myself,
So that I forgive my brother,
So that I Love myself,
So that I Love the world.

❧ MOLD ME ❧

I'm the clay in your hands, my Lord,
I'm the clay in your Holy Spirit, my Lord,
I'm the clay, I'm the clay!
Mold this cup of my essence to be pure love,
So that it may run over,
So I may be filled, and everyone may drink from me,
That I may bless my perceived enemies,
And surely, my loved ones,
That I may quench the thirst of my sisters, the trees,
The birds, and my four legged brothers,
All that You have created.
Make me that true oasis,
Let me become the Waters of Hope within Your Cup.
O mold me in life, in your sweetness,
In your everlasting compassion.

❧ SERENADE ❧

You come to me in my dreams.
The nights become days
And the love grows stronger than the gentleness of orchids,
I become the iron that you mold under your fire,
I long for the essence of the purified gold,
But You tell me that I am a Willow tree,
So my gaze goes into the forest,
Here I am, You molded me as a sparrow,
My flight is short, for my neighbor awoke me.
I'll look for You in her eyes without forgetting my chirping cry,
The One that will serenade, my Muse, my Creator, my Beloved.

℘ FIRE ℘

I see Your eyes through the fire,

You stare at me through the fire,

I am the fire,

And I am the staring,

My beloved Creator, You alone see me completely,

I see you,

The voices of my existence try to blind me,

But You, O Great Almighty, call me deeper than my breath,

I listen, and even to my friend,

The melancholy music, the melody of senses,

I say nay, nay,

For my Father is blessing me,

I will melt to His love,

I will melt in His Fire.

❧ CELL ❧

When you come to visit me in my cell,

Are you expecting to see waterfalls in my eyes?

Or perhaps my essence, drowning in the depth of a deep lake?

Or my longing swimming in the waters of an unnamed ocean?

Hold your judgment and expectations back, sweet brother,

And have a drink from my deepest well,

Taste my suffering while I tear my garments,

For your visit is a blessing

Only when we dance with the same, deeper tides,

And your open heart accepts my nakedness,

And so, together, we'll rejoice,

We'll celebrate the Presence of God,

Though all of it might unsettle you.

❦ I AM ❧

Where are you going? ... I am coming here.
When will you be arriving?...I will arrive now.
Who will you be finding? ... I will be meeting myself.
And I will kiss God...
And He will embrace me,
For He always was,
And so He is and always will be,
The Great I AM.

❧ THE DIVINE RIVERS ❧

Look left, look right, there, here!
Jump in ecstasy, my brother!
The rivers run wild, inviting you to jump in,
Jump in! Let yourself be free in the current of Pure Love,
The waters of the deep drowning you with the Breath of Life.
Soak yourself in the ten thousand questions of nothingness,
For you'll receive the answers of the Fullness of Life.
Look, look! It's you, it's you, my brother, what a divine sight!

ℰ REJOICING ℜ

On which side travels the soul?

Everywhere, I must say,

In autumn, in winter,

In marriage and birth,

He always was and is.

Contemplate the silence within the silence,

Fret not on questions about the presence of Eternal Love,

It's here, not there,

Rejoice, simple man, rejoice.

❧ THE STORM ❧

Every storm comes bearing gifts,
In my gentle humanness I may recoil in fear,
But He, the Beloved, whispers valiantly,
•You have been where you are for so long my child,
Come closer, come closer,
I yearn for you, my precious little one."
Allow the storm to bless you,
For Divinity you are, Divinity you become,
Closer and closer.
The calm has arrived.
Thank you.
Gentle smile,
It's okay.
As in all things, this too shall pass.

❧ THE UNFOLDING ❧

How much Love unfolds?

From these leaves on old oak trees,

The depth of canyon's spirits

Where the wind bathes his soul,

The lakes of murmuring silence

Where the loud voice is still in her unconscious,

How much Love unfolds?

In the nakedness of the moment,

The cry of the wilderness blinds the most ruthless man,

A child awakens in a mother wolf's breast,

Janus finds her sister's face in herself,

How much Love unfolds in this sacred heart now!

❧ THE PIERCING ❧

If it must be a dagger that will pierce me,
So that the sunburst of Your love
May emanate within me forever,
Pierce me, O my Beloved.
If it must be that darkness engulf me
So that the sunlight of Your Spirit may open me,
Let me fall into that abyss of blindness
So that Your Presence may be within me always.

❦ THE BEATING ❦

They tear me apart,
One pulls on my left arm,
Another kicks my stomach,
My heart is pierced by yet another,
My head thrown right and left in blows.
I'm alone,
All alone.
Who are these tyrants that assault me so viciously?
From where and when have I been sentenced to such punishment?
All alone, tears flow down.
I look at my assailant in the mirror,
He wants to offer me pity,
I'll take it.
I look for God in his eyes,
He whispers, "Love thyself, forgive thyself, embrace thyself."
I smile, I do, I smile, hopeful,
I crawl from a kick in the groin.

❧ EMPTY ❧

Lord, my inspiration is running out,

Am I existing solely out of my ego?

If so, kill me now,

Kill me completely,

So that I can be in Your light, or hide in Your shadow.

For I have been a sinner for so long

That I believe the sin to be a virtue

While my brothers and sisters smile at me,

Do they believe me,

Or do they smile out of pity for the broken delusional man?

Christ, Christ, O Christ, strike me with Your Spirit,

Let every cell of my body be taken with Your truth

Or else let the mere thought of my existence disappear completely in

the hereafter.

Amen.

ℰ THE GUEST IN MY TEMPLE ℱ

These friends of mine, visiting my temple,

This temple I cover with my aging skin,

They are many, these friends,

And some of them, I do know their names.

There's Mr. Anger, and Mrs. Jealousy, and Mrs. Depression, and Mr. Doubt,

And also Mr. Joy, and Mrs. Trust, Mrs. Gladness and Mr. Gratitude,

And so many more, these guests, so many!

How did they come and stay, surely I invited them,

And when do they leave and go, surely I say until next season.

Clouds in a vast sky, ever changing forms,

And to them I must say "thank you" and "yes,"

And bless them with Your presence, Father of Light,

And embrace the sweetness of the whole human experience.

❦ Us ❧

You in me, me in You
Your breath in me, my breath in You
Your life in me, my life in You
Of myself I am nothing
In You I am everything, my loving Christ.

❦ WILD HORSE ❦

In the veils of doubt I lost my innocence,

The pursuit of life as a wild horse in the plains,

Grazed on the green, drank from the rivers,

Slept to the lullabies of nurturing mother,

Then I questioned.

And the floods of desperation gripped my gallop,

I became a slave of my own questioning.

The sun rests and rises,

Yes, to the learning I found the path,

Until I lose it again only to come back home to my stable.

❦ THE MUSICIAN ❦

Father of Light,
That man, he played Your song,
The tears poured from his eccentric instrument,
His body convulsed with the melody,
No, it was no melody, it was a crying prayer,
A plea to the heavens.
Every note cried Jesuha Jesuha Jesuha
My heart wept with him,
Without seeing me, he thanked me.
I thanked him.
You thanked us.

❧ CROSSROADS ❧

These shadows, oh Lord,
Shed the Divine Healing Light on me.
For the darkness appears sweet and alluring,
And I'm blinded by her beauty.
How human am I!
While pursuing You, my Lord,
I built these crossroads with my own mind,
And romance my own death in open eyes,
I am weak, and I fall,
Be the Beam again, my Lord, I'm willing.

❦ SAILOR ❦

As a sailor I sailed the rivers if my blood,
As a drifter I conquer the streets of my soul,
As a farmer I sowed the storms of my anger,
As a man I kneel to the mercy of Forgiveness.

❧ WILLINGNESS ❧

And so it is that my Master asks of me:
•Are you willing to take all that comes with it•
And so it was that for many lives I said yes
When I wanted to say no.
And the waves of regret crumbled and crippled me,
And I crawled until I found You, my Loving Creator.
Somehow I knew to say a living Yes,
Because You live in all things,
And I get to be in You in all things.
And so it is that at this moment,
And the next moment,
And the next,
The Master's voice will sound from within again:
•Are you willing to take all that comes with it?•
And, awakened to this moment,
In infinite Love and Gratitude, I say Yes, Yes, Yes....

❧ RECOGNITION ☙

I saw You.
In the eyes of my sister, I saw You.
In the hands of a carpenter, I saw You.
Under the Bodhi Tree, I saw You.
In the lotus flower, I saw You.
In the synagogue, I saw You,
And in the Temple, and in Church I did, I saw You!
In the mirror,
In the mirror... I saw You.

❧ MUCH LOVE ❧

Day and night, night and day,
The streaming voice of Your Silence surrenders my will,
I die to myself, I die to myself.
I have drunk from the fountain of Love,
My swollen feet rest from the running,
My breath ends in murmur,• I love You• •I love You•
Everyone thinks I've gone mad,
Yes, I have,
I have gone mad in love for You, my loving Christ.

❧ THE SHOUTING ❧

I shout, I shout,
I'm the river, I'm the river!
Living waters, stillness, and existence,
I'm the breath of life,
And the space between the leaves,
Where the wind kisses me, and the rains adore me,
I delve in You, Great Spirit,
You within me, oh my Beloved Christ,
I shout, I am Love, I am Love!
I AM, I AM! For HE IS,
And He is in me,
And I rejoice.

❧ Joyful Becoming ❧

Joy, Joy, Joy
My Master is within me,
A fool, a sinner,
A lost soul, now a Winner
Oh my sweet Beloved,
I was a dry seed brought to life,
I was a barren woman and became a mother,
I was the night thief and now the giver.
I have found my love, You, my God,
You alone chose me,
Oh, tears of Joy, Joy, Joy

❧ YOUR GAZE ❧

Your gaze, my Beloved,
I lost the oceans in the sight of distant lands,
And I craved waters that spoke of love,
Now, in another well, I seek to quench my thirst,
But again I find it dry.
The Dove up above flew very near,
I believed I could see You clearly,
Maybe I've become delirious
But in Your reflection, the windows of my eternal soul,
Yes, I remember now, even as I walked as a child,
In those very eyes,
And such sweet gentle eyes I had!
In there, my Beloved, I found Your gaze,
And so I found You again,
Oh, no gentle look exists,
The shining of Your Light.
In Your waters I satisfied my soul,
I smiled, I smile
In this ecstasy, I contemplate You in my reflection.
As I drink my tears, I smile
Sweet freedom, my Beloved,
Your sweetness is everlasting.
I am whole.

❦ THE FLOWER ❧

Be a flower, my brother
Be a flower, my sweet brother
Be the essence of Love,
The fragrance of the Beloved.
Be of service to the bees
And the visitations of the wind
The kisses of the sun
And the blessings of the rain.
Feel the mastery of the earth
The eternity of being.
When one becomes a hammer,
Everything becomes a nail,
And all purpose becomes will
The very will that will ravish the soul with darkness and loneliness
Until one becomes a nail himself
All piercing, all coldness, rigidity
Oh, but soften your heart, sweet brother,
Loosen your grip,
Bend your stem,
Be a flower.
Be a flower.

❦ BELONGING ❦

I laid all that I was, am, and will be at Your feet,
You reject me not.
The cry of the eagle
Brought the awakening of my truth
I walk now, not in me, but in Your Mystery.
I see through, and taste the density of Your Divinity
In all that is, and in all that I am.
The rivers of being settle in my heart,
The vastness of Your Existence as been manifested in all,
I'm here, I'm yours, joyous to belong,
Joyous that I am.

❧ JOURNEY ❧

Before your thought of dust,
Your promise of love was already.
And so I took the journey to find You.
In the troubled canyons I felt You, and I said Thank You.
In the sorrowful oceans I felt You, and I said Thank You.
In the longing of the four winds I felt You, and I said Thank You.
In the whole that is life
In her magnificent landscapes, I felt You, and I said Thank You.
In the exhaustion of my humanness, I became.
And I sat, and there I met me.
And I stayed, and it hurt, and I felt so lost, but remained.
And I heard You say Thank You.
And the dust that I am became the Love that You Are.

9 780615 564074